Say It, Don't Spray It!

by Lexi Parker

Illustrations by Rose Bennington

For the families I've been lucky enough to work with.

Your effort, resilience, and love inspire me everyday.

More of your favorite characters from this series of books

Bob

Petey

Ralphie

Lana the llama lived on Lone Star Ranch with her livestock family and friends.

She loved to play Lasso the Leader, laze about,
and catch lightning bugs on warm summer nights.

Lana was a lovely llama, but there was just one problem…
Lana would forget to use her words. She would spray it instead of say it.

One day she was playing Lasso the Leader with her friends.
Lucy decided to be the leader when Lana wanted to be the leader.

Lana opened her mouth and sprayed it, instead of saying it.
"Yuck! Now I need to go take a bath!" Lucy exclaimed. "Come on everyone,
let's go," and her friends sprinted off, leaving Lana all alone.

Later when Lana went to laze about in the lupine field,
her friend Leo laid down in the spot that she was going to lay in.

Lana sprayed it instead of saying it. "Gross Lana," cried Leo.
"I'm leaving!" and Leo trotted off leaving Lana alone once again.

When Lana woke up, the lightning bugs were flashing all around.
She ran to get her jar, but Mama Llama was still washing it.

Lana wanted the jar and sprayed it instead of saying it.
Mama Llama turned around soaking wet. "Lana!
Now you can't go lightning bug catching at all tonight," she scolded.

Lana sobbed away to her stall.
She had sprayed it instead of saying it all day and missed out on all of the fun.

The next morning Lana got up and was leaving her stall when Mama Llama asked to talk. "Lana, when you want something say it, don't spray it. If you spray it instead of using your words, no one will know what you want."

"How can I remember to use my words?" asked Lana. That's easy,
as soon as you want something, stop, take a deep breath,
and remind yourself no one knows what you want unless you say it."
"Okay, I'll try Mama," and off she galloped to meet her friends.

Lana and her friends were playing Lasso the Leader when Lana wanted a turn.
She was just about to spray it, but then remembered what Mama Llama had said.
She stopped, took a deep breath, and reminded herself that her friends won't
know what she wants unless she says it.
"Can I be the leader this time?" Lana asked.

"Of course!" her friends happily replied.
Lana bolted off smiling as Louie and Lucy chased her with the lasso.

After a long day of lassoing, Lana felt exhausted. She trotted over to laze about in the lupine field and saw Leo in her spot. She stopped, took a deep breath, and reminded herself that Leo won't know what she wants unless she says it. "Can I laze here too?" "Sure," said Leo. Lana laid down and dozed off with a smile on her face.

When Lana woke up she saw the flashes of lightning bugs throughout the night sky. She quickly stood up and ran to get her jar.

When Lana got home she couldn't find her jar anywhere and was just about to spray it, when she realized Mama wouldn't know what she wanted if she did. She stopped and took a deep breath. "Mama, where is my jar?"

Mama Llama lovingly nestled her nose to Lana. "You used your words Lana! I'm so proud of you! You can catch lightning bugs for an extra hour tonight." And she handed her the jar.

"Wow! Saying it is way more fun than spraying it,"
giggled Lana as she trotted off to go play with her friends.

THE END

www.ingramcontent.com/pod-product-compliance
Lightning Source LLC
Chambersburg PA
CBHW041243040426

42445CB00004B/135

* 9 7 8 0 9 8 5 1 2 5 6 2 2 *